WHAT IS A MOON?

RYAN NAGELHOUT

Britannica
Educational Publishing

IN ASSOCIATION WITH

ROSEN
EDUCATIONAL SERVICES

Published in 2015 by Britannica Educational Publishing (a trademark of Encyclopædia Britannica, Inc.) in association with The Rosen Publishing Group, Inc.
29 East 21st Street, New York, NY 10010

Distributed exclusively by Rosen Publishing.
To see additional Britannica Educational Publishing titles, go to rosenpublishing.com.

First Edition

Britannica Educational Publishing
J.E. Luebering: Director, Core Reference Group
Mary Rose McCudden: Editor, Britannica Student Encyclopedia

Rosen Publishing
Hope Lourie Killcoyne: Executive Editor
Editor: Kathy Kuhtz Campbell
Nelson Sá: Art Director
Designer: Brian Garvey
Cindy Reiman: Photography Manager
Photo Researcher: Amy Feinberg

Cataloging-in-Publication Data

Nagelhout, Ryan, author.
What is a moon?/Ryan Nagelhout. — First edition.
     pages cm. — (Let's find out! Space)
Includes bibliographical references and index.
ISBN 978-1-62275-466-3 (library bound) — ISBN 978-1-62275-468-7 (pbk.) — ISBN 978-1-62275-469-4 (6-pack)
1. Satellites — Juvenile literature. 2. Moon — Juvenile literature. 3. Solar system — Juvenile literature. I. Title.
QB582.N34 2015
523.9'8 — dc23
                                                                                                  2013048384

Manufactured in the United States of America

CONTENTS

UP IN THE SKY

What do you see when you look up in the night sky? With no clouds, you can see many bright stars. The brightest object in the night sky is not a star. It is Earth's Moon.

Since people first walked on Earth, they have studied the Moon.

A moon is a satellite, which is an object that orbits a larger object. Moons orbit planets and other large bodies because of gravity. Gravity is a force that attracts objects to the mass of other things. Planets orbit stars, such as the Sun, but moons are caught in the gravity of planets.

Every planet in Earth's solar system except Mercury and Venus has at least one moon that scientists know about.

Earth's gravity keeps the Moon in orbit around our home planet.

THINK ABOUT IT
New moons are always being discovered by scientists. Why do you think Mercury and Venus do not have any moons?

Moon, Satellite, or Planet?

Today, there are many satellites orbiting Earth. Humans made all but one of these satellites. They put these machines into space for various reasons. Earth has only one natural satellite: the Moon.

The ancient Greeks called Earth's Moon a "planet." To them a planet was anything big and bright

The Hubble Space Telescope is a human-made satellite that orbits Earth.

THINK ABOUT IT

The International Space Station (ISS) is a satellite that orbits Earth. What is the difference between the ISS and the Moon?

that moved in the sky. This belief meant that a star such as the Sun was a planet but Earth was not.

In the 1600s, the invention of the telescope let people observe the Moon and the rest of space more carefully. Now people know there are many moons in the solar system, and there may be many more throughout the universe.

When seen from the Moon, Earth appears to be in one spot all the time.

7

EARTH'S MOON

The diameter of the Moon is a little more than one-quarter the size of the diameter of Earth. Its diameter, or distance through its center, is about 2,200 miles (3,500 kilometers). The Moon is made mostly of rock.

The Moon is bright because it reflects the Sun's light.

In this kind of eclipse, a thin outer ring of the Sun's disk is not covered by the Moon's dark disk.

On average, it orbits about 238,900 miles (384,400 km) from Earth.

Like the planets, the Moon has two types of movement: orbit and spin. It takes the Moon about 27 days to make one trip around Earth. The Moon also spins about its center. It completes one rotation in about 27 days. Because the Moon takes about the same amount of time to complete one orbit and one rotation, the same side of the Moon always faces Earth. The Moon does not give off light. It reflects light coming from the Sun.

An event called a total solar eclipse occurs when the Moon passes between Earth and the Sun. The Moon blocks all but the outline of the Sun for a short time.

CRATERS AND PLAINS

The surface of the Moon has thousands of pits called craters. The craters form when chunks of rock and metal called meteorites crash into the Moon. These crashes have covered the Moon's surface with rocks and dust. The Moon also has plains made of lava that erupted from volcanoes billions of years ago. It has its own gravity, but it is less than Earth's.

Through the ages people have thought that the crater-and-plain pattern of the Moon's surface as seen from Earth looked like a face. They called it "the man in the Moon."

The Moon's smaller craters were formed by meteor impacts, while the larger ones were created by collisions with asteroids.

Meteorites have changed the face of the Moon because it does not have an atmosphere to protect it. The absence of an atmosphere also leads to a wide range of temperatures on the Moon. During the daytime, when the Moon faces the Sun, its surface temperature is about 225°F (107°C). At night, the temperature drops to about -243°F (-153°C).

Tides are created in part by the action of the Moon's gravity when it pulls on Earth's seas, causing the water to rise and fall every day.

How Earth's Moon Formed

Moons can be formed in many ways. Scientists are not entirely sure how Earth's Moon was formed, but they do have ideas. The leading idea is that a large rock crashed into Earth. This rock broke off part of the planet, which became the Moon.

THINK ABOUT IT
Scientists know the Moon is made of rocks similar to those on Earth. How do you think the Moon was formed?

Most scientists believe the Moon was created about 4.5 billion years ago.

Another idea is that both Earth and the Moon were formed together around the same time. Some scientists believe the Moon was formed somewhere else and later got pulled in by Earth's gravity. However, these ideas can't explain how Earth and the Moon have similar rocks.

In 1969, astronauts from the United States first visited the Moon to study it. Twelve people have walked on its surface since then.

Some scientists think the Moon was formed when an object, which they named Theia, hit Earth.

Moons of Mars

Mars is the fourth planet from the Sun. It has two known moons, Phobos and Deimos. Astronomer Asaph Hall discovered them in 1877. Both moons are small and have low gravity. Phobos is about 16.5 miles (26.6 km) long at its longest point. Deimos is about 9 miles (15 km) long at its longest point. They are both shaped like potatoes.

Phobos is very close to Mars. It is about 5,825 miles (9,375 km) from the planet's

Mars is called the Red Planet because it has a reddish color in the sky.

THINK ABOUT IT
Phobos and Deimos are very small. Why do you think Mars's moons are not round?

Deimos completes one orbit around Mars in about 30 Earth hours.

center. Mars's gravity is so strong that Phobos will someday crash into the planet's surface. One of Phobos's craters, named Stickney, is about half as wide as Phobos itself.

Jupiter and Ganymede

Jupiter is the fifth planet from the Sun. It is mostly made of gases, and it is the first of the planets called "gas giants." It has more than 60 known moons. Astronomers on Earth using large telescopes have been searching for more. In 1610, Jupiter's four brightest moons were the first space objects discovered by astronomer Galileo Galilei with a telescope. Those moons were named Ganymede, Io, Europa, and Callisto.

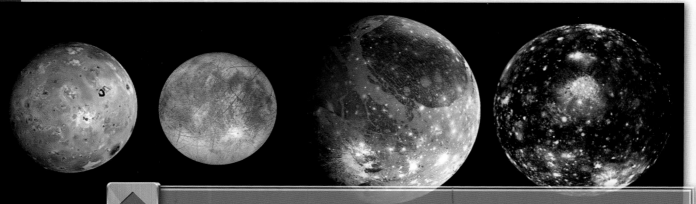

The four largest moons of Jupiter—Io, Europa, Ganymede, and Callisto—are called Galilean satellites in Galileo's honor.

Ganymede has
an iron-rich core.
Scientists believe
Earth's inner
core is made
mostly of iron.

THINK ABOUT IT
Many rocks form an
asteroid belt between the
orbits of Mars and Jupiter.
Why don't scientists call
these rocks moons?

Ganymede is the
largest moon in the solar
system. It is larger than the
planet Mercury. Its iron
core creates its own magnetic field. Its surface is very
icy and may have water under it. Io has gigantic, active
volcanoes on its surface.

SATURN AND TITAN

Saturn is a gas giant and the sixth planet from the Sun. Saturn has more than 60 moons. Titan is Saturn's largest moon

Saturn's many moons vary greatly in size.

and the second largest in the solar system. Discovered in 1655, it was the first moon found after Jupiter's first four moons were discovered. It is the only moon that has clouds. Its atmosphere is made of thick gases such as nitrogen and methane. It also has lakes of ethane on its surface.

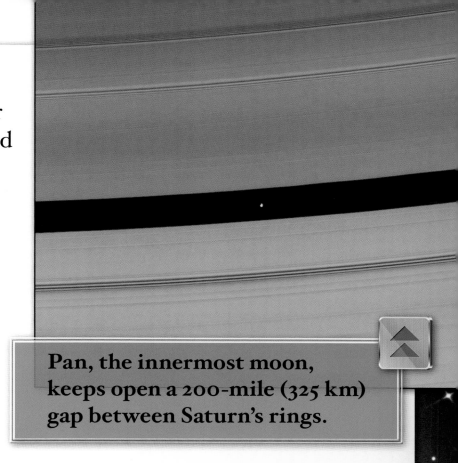

Pan, the innermost moon, keeps open a 200-mile (325 km) gap between Saturn's rings.

Saturn's rings are made of ice and rock but are not moons. However, many small moons help keep the rings in place. The moon Pan was discovered in 1990 between two of the rings. Other moons like Pan keep the edges of nearby rings sharp and distinct.

Uranus and Miranda

Uranus is the seventh planet from the Sun. It has 27 known moons. Its five major moons are Oberon, Titania, Ariel, Umbriel, and Miranda. Uranus's other moons are very small. Eight of the small moons are so close together that

The two largest moons of Uranus, Oberon and Titania, were discovered by William Herschel in 1787.

COMPARE AND CONTRAST

Compare and contrast the shape of Miranda and Earth's Moon. What is different about the two moons?

scientists are not sure how they avoid crashing into one another. Scientists think all of Uranus's moons are made of frozen water and rock.

Miranda, like most of Uranus's moons, was named after a character in a play by William Shakespeare.

Miranda is the smallest of the major moons. Its surface is very strange. It has some spots with huge craters. Other areas have big valleys and cliffs. It looks like many pieces of rock and ice were smashed together. Miranda may have been broken apart by crashing into other objects, then put back together again.

Neptune's Moons

Neptune is the farthest planet from the Sun. It has 13 known moons. Its largest is named Triton. Triton was discovered in 1846, about a month after scientists found Neptune. Triton is nearly as big as Earth's Moon.

Scientists believe that Triton might have formed as an independent planet. Because of gravity, Neptune may have pulled Triton into its orbit. Unlike all the other large moons in the solar system, Triton revolves around

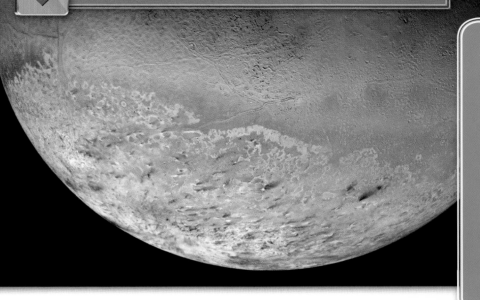

the planet in a direction opposite to Neptune's spin. Nereid was discovered in 1949. Its orbit is the most oval-shaped of all the known moons in the solar system. Scientists believe Nereid is a captured asteroid. Its orbit also could have been changed when Triton was captured by Neptune's gravity.

What About Pluto?

Pluto is a dwarf planet that was discovered in 1930. First thought to be a planet, it was downgraded by scientists in 2006. It now belongs to a group of rocks and asteroids at the edge of the solar system called the Kuiper Belt.

Pluto has five moons. Charon, with a diameter of nearly 750 miles (1,210 km), was discovered in 1978. Nix and Hydra followed in 2005. A fourth moon, Kerberos, was found in 2011. A fifth moon was named Styx in 2013.

Charon is located very close to Pluto. It was partly hidden by the glare of Pluto's light until 1978.

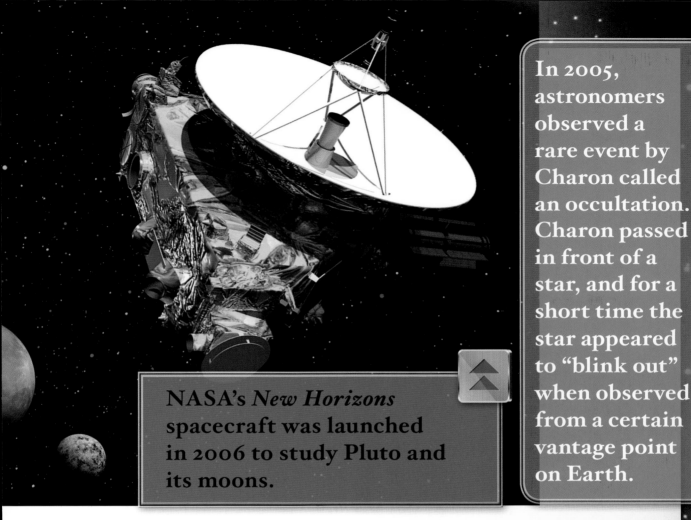

In 2005, astronomers observed a rare event by Charon called an occultation. Charon passed in front of a star, and for a short time the star appeared to "blink out" when observed from a certain vantage point on Earth.

NASA's *New Horizons* spacecraft was launched in 2006 to study Pluto and its moons.

Pluto and Charon are closer in size than any of the planets and their moons. Scientists are always discovering new bodies in the Kuiper Belt. Although none are considered planets, many of them have moons.

Ida and Dactyl

Scientists have even found asteroids with their own moons. In 1884, astronomer Johann Palisa discovered an asteroid that he named Ida. The *Galileo* spacecraft passed Ida in 1993 and took pictures of it. Scientists noticed a small rock actually orbiting Ida. It was the first moon discovered that orbited

Think About It

Moons can orbit anything that has its own gravity. Do you think a moon could have its own moon?

When it was first discovered, Ida was called "Asteroid 243."

The *Galileo* spacecraft has also visited an asteroid called Gaspra.

something other than a planet. They named the moon Dactyl, after a group of beings from Greek mythology who lived on Mount Ida.

A tiny speck in photographs, Dactyl is 1 mile (1.6 km) at its widest point. It orbits about 56 miles (90 km) away from Ida. Scientists have since discovered about 20 other moons orbiting asteroids. The moons have helped scientists determine the density of these asteroids.

NEW MOONS

Humans once called the Moon a planet but now know of more than 145 named moons. Today, people know moons are bodies that orbit planets and objects other than stars. Some moons are just rocks, while others are made of ice. One

The sixth landing of humans on the Moon was *Apollo 17* in 1972.

THINK ABOUT IT
Humans have not walked on Earth's Moon since 1972. Do you think people should go back to visit the Moon?

监视相机C图像

In December 2013, China landed its first spacecraft on the Moon.

moon, Titan, has its own atmosphere. As humans explore the solar system they find other moons and learn more about them.

The definition of what a moon can be is always changing as scientists learn new things. As people explore deeper into space, they find more moons orbiting planets. They may even find moons outside the solar system.

GLOSSARY

asteroid belt A group of asteroids orbiting the Sun between Mars and Jupiter.

astronomer A scientist that studies space.

atmosphere A mass of gases surrounding a body.

craters Bowl-shaped holes on the surface of a planet or moon.

density How much mass is in a certain volume.

gravity The force that pulls objects toward the center of a body.

international Involving two or more countries.

Kuiper Belt A group of icy bodies at the edge of our solar system.

meteorites Pieces of rock or metal that have fallen from space to the ground; meteors that have reached the surface of Earth without burning up.

myth A story that was told in ancient culture to explain a practice, belief, or natural happening.

orbit The path taken by a body circling around another body.

reflects Gives back light.

revolves Spins.

rotation One complete turn.

satellite A natural or human-made object that orbits Earth, the Moon, or another heavenly body.

spacecraft Vehicles designed for travel beyond Earth's atmosphere.

telescope A tool that makes faraway objects look bigger and closer.

temperatures Measurements that indicate how hot or cold something is.

universe All of space and everything in it including stars, planets, galaxies, etc.

volcanoes Openings in a planet's or moon's surface through which hot liquid rock or ice sometimes flows.

For More Information

Books

Higgins, Nadia. *The Solar System Through Infographics*. Minneapolis, MN: Lerner Publications, 2014.

Lawrence, Ellen. *The Moon: Our Neighbor in Space*. Cornwall, England: Ruby Tuesday Books, 2014.

Owen, Ruth. *Saturn*. New York, NY: Windmill Books, 2014.

Shereda, Laura. *Spectacular Space Trivia*. New York, NY: Gareth Stevens Publishing, 2014.

Squire, Ann. *Planet Mars*. New York, NY: Children's Press, 2014.

Taylor-Butler, Christine. *Jupiter*. New York, NY: Children's Press, 2014.

Websites

Because of the changing nature of Internet links, Rosen Publishing has developed an online list of websites related to the subject of this book. This site is updated regularly. Please use this link to access the list:

http://www.rosenlinks.com/lfo/moon

Index